For Kate

Designed and illustrated by Sara Lynn
Design assistance Claire Legemah
With thanks to Cliff Moon, Barry Macey and
Alison Boyle

First published in Great Britain in 1988 by
Two-Can Publishing Limited
27 Cowper Street
London EC2A 4AP

© **Sara Lynn 1988**

Reproduction by Colourscan, Singapore
Printed and bound by Dai Nippon, Hong Kong

British Library Cataloguing in Publication Data

Lynn, Sara,
Noises.
1. English language. Readers – For pre-school children
I. Title
428.6

ISBN 1-85434-020-4
ISBN 1-85434-030-1 Pbk

Noises

Sara Lynn

TWO-CAN

tick tock

boing
boing

ring-ding
ring-ding

doi-oing!

bzzz

zoom

bzzz
bzzz

bzzz

whizzz...

cuckoo
cuckoo

snip
snip

slosh!

ding-a-ling-
a-ling

What sound goes with each picture?
Which are quiet sounds and which are loud sounds?

bang clang

eek eek

ring ding

snip snip

Are these animals below making the right noises?
Do you know what noise each animal should make?